The Devilish Dialogues

Advocates Of Good And Evil Debate The Parables Of Jesus

Arthur A. Rouner, Jr.
– The Lord's Advocate

Maurice A. Fetty
– The Devil's Advocate

CSS Publishing Company, Inc., Lima, Ohio

THE DEVILISH DIALOGUES

For more information about CSS Publishing Company resources, visit our website at www.csspub.com or e-mail us at custserv@csspub.com or call (800) 241-4056.

ISBN 0-7880-1939-2 PRINTED IN U.S.A.

These dialogues, raising the issues of good and evil as the voices of our time, are dedicated to those Sunday evening congregations of The Colonial Church of Edina, who came to hiss and boo and cheer, and so learn the stark issues of life and death, and came to understand and recognize the persuasive voice of evil in tempting times. By their delight and enthusiasm, they greatly encouraged the attempt of two young ministers to teach through dramatic dialogue in a winsome way. Bless 'em all.

Table Of Contents

Preface

The "Devilish Dialogues" originally were created for the Lenten Vesper Series at the Colonial Church of Edina (Community Congregational) in Minneapolis, Minnesota. The Reverend Dr. Arthur A. Rouner, Jr., and The Reverend Maurice A. Fetty, Preaching Minister and Teaching Minister, respectively, conceived the series as a new approach to communicating the Christian message. Fetty wrote and played the part of the Devil's Advocate; Rouner wrote and played the part of the Lord's Advocate.

Congregations sometimes grow restive with the monologue sermon. Some people want to raise questions or talk back, or present a varying point of view. The dialogue approach enabled Rouner and Fetty to delineate more graphically opposing points of view.

Some were restive that the Devil "should be given his due," right in church even! Others welcomed the "no holds barred" approach in the effort to "tell it like it really is."

Others were glad to have the message of the Lord's Advocate set in stark contrast to the enticements of the Devil's Advocate. Whatever the sentiments, the "Devilish Dialogues" became a very popular Lenten Vesper Series at the Colonial Church of Edina.

Rouner and Fetty went on to give some of the Dialogues on WCCO Television in Minneapolis and in other settings. The television station experienced high audience response from the series.

The "Devilish Dialogues" are presented here for personal stimulation and possible emulation in churches, chapels, classrooms, and retreat settings throughout the nation.

Introduction

Jesus was a master storyteller. Whether in a few words or in a longer narrative, he gave insights and conveyed truths which have guided and inspired the Christian Church for centuries.

The stories were and are memorable. The first generation of hearers were so impressed they committed them to memory and wrote them down for hundreds of succeeding generations. Images from the stories such as the "ten virgins" or the "four kinds of soil" are familiar to many.

And the "prodigal son" story seems to be known almost worldwide, probably because its truth is experienced so universally. It is with good reason it often has been called "the world's greatest short story."

The parables, or short stories, of Jesus have expressed timeless truths for centuries. It is our hope that they will take on new life and meaning in these "Devilish Dialogues."

Arthur A. Rouner, Jr. — The Lord's Advocate
Maurice A. Fetty — The Devil's Advocate

The Prodigal Son

So he returned home to his father. And while he was still a long distance away, his father saw him coming, and was filled with loving pity and ran and embraced him and kissed him.

His son said to him, "Father, I have sinned against heaven and against you, and am not worthy of being called your son...."

But his father said to the slaves, "Quick! Bring the finest robe in the house and put it on him. And a jeweled ring for his finger; and shoes! And kill the calf we have in the fattening pen. We must celebrate with a feast, for this son of mine was dead and has returned to life. He was lost and is found." So the party began.

— Luke 15:20-24

I

The Devil's Advocate:

Right at the beginning, I wish to make at least one thing clear: I am at a distinct disadvantage having to speak here in this church with all these religions trappings. Look at it: lighted candles, high altar, soft lights, and emotional music. Religious sentiment is hanging out all over.

So, I want you to know that I have to make my appeal through all the glut of sentimentalism, nostalgia, and religious wishful thinking. Furthermore, I want to point out that most people check their intelligence the minute they enter the church door. It is almost as if they had an intelligence rack alongside the coat and hat rack, so that every time they hang up their coat they hang up their intelligence as well. Once that's done, they enter the sanctuary and sit in a half-somnolent state waiting to be titillated with pious mishmash and soothed with illusory dream-spinning about how they wished everything might be, without ever letting any fact of harsh reality trouble their delicate little minds and hearts. So you see, I am usually at quite a disadvantage.

But probably not here in this church. For as I look out across the congregation, I am aware that I am in the company of intelligent men and women, dedicated to sorting out fact from fancy, reality from idealism, actuality from illusion. It is encouraging, for I am persuaded that balanced, cool-headed, reasonable people such as yourselves will see the rightness and reasonableness of my argument. Your superior intelligence and logical brilliance will be a great asset in warding off the idealistic pitch which my perennial opponent will be throwing at you. So in that respect, I feel very fortunate to be able to address you, even though we are not in neutral territory.

The Lord's Advocate:

We think you're putting us on, Devil's Advocate. After all, soft lights and flickering candles set a pretty good scene for you, too! What could be more tempting, after all, than to turn piety into patronage, sentimentality into self-interest, soft lighting into a soft sell — for hell?

You're at no disadvantage! Even if these "trappings" you speak of do mean something a little more to us than you seem to think, and go a little deeper than you might imagine.

Those tapers, with their flame, friend, tell us the Holy Spirit of our Lord is here. He comes like fire, to burn in our hearts — a fire you may have trouble drowning out. And that cross is where our Christ was crucified. He loves us — and you, too, tempting one — enough to give his life. That's a lot to do. Can you match that?

The lights are low, because it's evening. There's healing in evening's glow, didn't you know? And we come for help. And you'll have to work awfully hard to keep us from getting it.

But — say on!

II

The Devil's Advocate:

This parable of the so-called Prodigal Son is one of the most unfair, sentimentalized pieces of religious mishmash that I have ever come across. Most everyone knows the story. There are all kinds of proverbial sayings about prodigal sons. But the Church has been terribly guilty of propagating half-truths and distorted points of view regarding this parable. Can you not just see the hauteur, the sneering snobbishness, with which they tell this story of the younger prodigal son? They sit on their comfortable self-righteousness like a Charles de Gaulle on Mount Olympus, viewing with contemptuous disdain the supposed excesses, follies, and failures of this wayward young man. They have terrible bias which prevents them from seeing the reality of the story. And what is the reality?

The reality is this: the younger son knew the real story of his sated old man and pompous older brother. The old man was probably a stuffy, stalemated, old-line capitalist, wedded to the old order of things. He was probably crotchety, unyielding, unbending, unwilling to see anything new or try anything different. He was fearful, rigid, unwilling to take a risk, afraid to learn anything or experience anything that might threaten his own small ideas or shake up his little fiefdom. His life was provincial, circumscribed, stale, arid, and dull.

Now, I ask you, who wouldn't want to leave a closed-in, stultifying place like that? Any young man with intelligence and drive and dreams would have to get out of a place like that. If he stayed around there he would become dull and sullen and indolent, just as his older brother had already. The younger brother saw that if he were going to make it in this world, he was going to have to get out on his own.

Besides, there are other little factors that people such as my opponent over there like to overlook as they tell the story from their biased point of view. You know, people always think the young son was crass and greedy by asking for his share of the inheritance in advance. But a closer look will tell you he was just shrewd, because the older son got twice as much inheritance as the younger. That's right, according to Jewish law, as recorded in Deuteronomy

21:17, the firstborn son gets twice as much inheritance as anyone else in the family. Now anybody, especially younger brothers, can tell you that's a lousy deal. What younger man would want to stay around under that kind of injustice? His older brother would always have the upper hand. The younger brother had no real chance for advancement, no real chance to come into his own. So, why shouldn't he get out?

Besides, there are a lot of older brothers who come off rather badly in history, especially in the Bible. Contrary to some of the superstitions of the firstborn being the best born, the one on whom the strength and therefore, the inheritance falls, the younger sons often come off better. Remember, it was Cain, the older brother, who in jealousy killed his more capable younger brother, Abel. Remember, too, how Esau hated his more clever, cunning, and younger brother, Jacob.

Older brothers have a tendency to be too much like their fathers. They are identified with the old order, the old way of thinking and doing. They always keep the old rules, color within the lines, and stay at home near Mommy and Daddy. They are unimaginative. And, because they have the financial and psychological advantage of the inheritance, they rarely try anything new, rarely take any creative initiative. Their future is in an inherited future, which is another way of saying that they will be a carbon copy of the past.

I say, "God bless ..." I mean, "Satan bless the younger brother." He saw things as they really were and he set out to do something different, to be his own man, to chart his own course. Listen, why should his whole life be one of accepting hand-me-downs from his less-than-brilliant older brother? Why should he be forever disadvantaged because of an accident of birth? Why should he not get out from under his stodgy father and his dull, bossy brother? I'm for the young man. He wanted to be free from the burdening oppressiveness of his father and brother.

The Lord's Advocate:

I'm for the young man, too! So was his father for the young man.

Funny, how that stuffy, narrow-minded, conservative, John Birch, Rotarian, dirty old capitalist-of-a-father suddenly has such a beautiful bridge across the generation gap, and listened to his swinging son without letting his hair stand on end, and understood what was really bugging the boy, and was able to hold out his arms in welcome and forgiveness, isn't it?

Would that more conservative, capitalist fathers in our congregation today had such humble hearts, and open understanding, and ears that hear toward the kids of today.

No, we pious types are not nearly so narrow-minded and condemning of the Prodigal Son as you seem to think.

Let's concede that second sons do get an unfair deal when it comes to inheritance. Maybe the boy did have good reasons for cutting out and putting up in his own pad in some city far away. I'm not sure many fathers today would give that big a chunk to any child to take off with and live it up. That forgiving father begins to look a lot like a liberal to me. Seemed to know this was the only way the lad would learn, learn that self-centeredness isn't something you can survive on.

I'm not sure that home really was such a bad place to live. But, whatever kind of home it was, nobody forced him to stay. He went with his father's blessing, a great deal of faith on his father's part, I'd say.

A good example for fathers to follow in our day. Let kids get out of the white suburban ghetto. Let them see what the world is like. Let them see the many colors people come it, the many streets other sons live on, the kinds of fathers other fellows have. It's different. And "learning by living" is still a pretty good way.

A wise and loving man, I'd say, to let number two son have his way.

III

The Devil's Advocate:

I'm for the young man, no matter what you say. He's the stuff the world is made of: spirit, intelligence, adventure, risk, ambition, and independence. Yes, sir, I'm for him. And I know many of you are, too. For the young man represents, in many ways, the

American spirit: independent, free, willing to go on its own and take its own risks.

You will notice that the younger son went into a far country. He didn't hang around to mooch off the family. There were no pleading letters home, no tearful, weepy scenes for his mommy. When he left, he left. If he was going to be a man, he was going to be a man. He didn't even hang around to make it off his relatives or his dad's business acquaintances. Instead, he left the country, went to a place where the culture and customs were different, the business world unfamiliar, and the people strangers.

Now, of course, like many young men, he ran into a little bad luck. You must remember that he had lived a rather drab and dull life up to now. He had been isolated, provincialized, and totally unacquainted with other people and other ways of life. He had lived in an ideal, homogeneous, upper middle-class ghetto. Life had been pleasant, but it was pleasantly bland, with no spice or challenge.

So, the first thing to remember is the excitement which must have been his when he got to the big city in that other country. He most likely went to the Paris or New York of his day. And it was a most expanding, eye-opening experience. He wondered how he could have waited so long to make the break with the old home for this new way of life.

One of the first things he wanted to try was the reputedly good vintage wine and gourmet cuisine of that city. So, he made the rounds. Italian, French, Chinese, Jewish, Russian, Japanese, Hungarian, and German restaurants became a regular part of his experience. And in the course of it, he picked up a few friends. After all, who wants to eat alone? They had some great times and he came to be regarded as a leading connoisseur of wines and foods. Some restaurants began to give him discounts because of his kindly recommendations in their behalf. He was, in the very best sense of the word, a cultured man. He had finesse, poise, class, style, and ... money.

But foods and wines are only part of the delightful experiences of a man of the world. There is also the world of women, and his adopted city was full of them: beautiful, clever, sexy, luscious, and willing.

The young man's own attitudes about women and sex were somewhat clouded and unsure, but he was confident he did not want to repeat either his father's or his brother's attitudes and experiences. In fact, he had come to believe that their pent-up sexual feelings and inhibitions were what made them so dull and lifeless.

He guessed that his father's wife was rather languid and pallid when it came to man-woman relationships, because the only time he ever noticed a change in her was when he slipped some rum into her cake. His older brother's wife was neurotic and frigid and was undoubtedly the reason he was so devoted to his work. He suspected that both his father and brother were probably quite desperate, and that was undoubtedly the explanation for their pinching of the cleaning lady and flirting with the maid. And if you could have seen the maid and cleaning lady you would realize even more how desperate they were.

Well, the younger brother rightly felt all that kind of conduct to be fake, phony, and futile. If a man is going to commit psychological adultery, he might as well do the real thing. Besides, he saw that the sexual mores of his father and brother were mostly bound up with the economic system. They needed a stable family unit to support the economic system and to provide legitimate heirs by which they would retain control.

But the young man was enlightened. He wanted to be free to experience the delights of the body. He wanted to divorce sex from the economic system. He wanted to be done with the hypocrisy of his brother and father. He wanted to be open, uninhibited, unhypocritical.

So, he subscribed to a magazine called *Bunny* and went to the right clubs and night spots, and made his way in this new world of experience. It was a grand life, full of pleasure, uninhibited, free: a journey of pure delight. It was the kind of life described by your magazines — you know, the ones your men have under their mattresses. He took the wraps off the old taboos. And, though not as promiscuous as your American groupies, who follow the rock bands and athletes around to keep their beds warm, he was not, on the other hand, as idealistic as your college kids who say they make love only when in love.

Rather, he saw sex as a gift to be enjoyed and satisfied, quite apart from empty moralisms and tight-knit economic systems. So it was that, contrary to the opinions of the puritanical moralists, our young man became a truly enlightened, liberated person, truly a man of the world.

The Lord's Advocate:

It does seem uncharitable to disagree. I'm sure the Prodigal Son was a nice boy, and perhaps he did become something of a culture buff in that far country, sampling the wines of the world and the dishes of the different countries, not to mention the female dishes that were evidently served up to him in response to the well-known fact that he had money to pay for his pleasures!

But it doesn't really say he was a symphony season ticket holder, or one of the theater group of first-nighters. If he was a sophisticate or a swinger, he evidently did his swinging at a pretty low level.

The scripture says that the young man "wasted all his money on parties and prostitutes." "Prodigal" means to waste, to throw away. I think your young man of the world was very young indeed, and rather immature, not a little selfish, and not very smart.

In fact, if he messed with prostitutes he was in an awfully big hurry for sex, wasn't he? Looks to me as though he couldn't wait to build a relationship with a woman, that he wasn't really interested in love, and that he certainly didn't find anyone to care about or care for.

Indeed, he was duped! The kind of so-called "friends" he collected were quite evidently people who were only interested in his money. As long as he had it, they were around. But, when he ran out, they dropped him like the proverbial hot potato.

When the famine came, he suddenly didn't have a friend anywhere! All of a sudden, nobody knew him. He, who had been a welcome guest as long as he had money, was now everyone's excess baggage. Nobody wanted him. He starved. He finally had to hire on with a farmer, until he found himself eating the pods that the pigs left.

He was used, manipulated, "taken." And the kind of blindness that allows that to happen is usually the blindness of selfishness. He had been so centered on himself that he never saw that these "friends" were only moochers, that these women were only predators who cared nothing for him as a person.

It's when selfishness rules the roost, and egotism dominates the heart, that sin sickens the soul, that a person's life gets out of tune, out of touch with the best that he knows, the best principles, the best people, the best hopes and dreams and ideals and goals.

And it was when he was good and hungry, tired and dirty, and without friends or funds, that he began to look back over his life and think about his family and look into his own heart, and, as the scripture says, "finally came to his senses."

He may have thought his fling was fine while it lasted. But he changed his mind. And, when he finally went home, he said, "Father, I have sinned...."

IV

The Devil's Advocate:

Now, my friends, I must confess that I am reluctant to discuss this last section of the parable with you. I know that you have been very sympathetic and understanding to our young man. You have seen the sheer folly and absurdity of our misguided moralist. His arguments have been vain and windy, unrealistic and pompous.

Therefore, I want you to understand that we are not conceding a thing to our defender of the status quo. But we shall have to admit that our young man failed us. He was our hero, the hope of our future generations, but alas, he was much more immature than we thought. Just when he was becoming a leading man of the world, a connoisseur of women and wine, he chickened out on us and ran for Daddy and home. I must admit that it is disgusting.

It is disgusting on at least two counts. The first is that, like an idiot, he spent all his money, rather than wisely investing it so it would be a constant source of independence for him. So when his money was gone, he didn't stand up and work like a man. Nor, did he exercise enough intelligence to con a good job out of his friends. Now, hardly anybody can tolerate that kind of stupidity. So, what does he do? He goes whining back to Daddy. He knows that at least his stodgy old dad will take him back as a slave.

So off he goes back home like a sobbing adolescent. And, what is worse, he even falls for his father's forgiveness line. We all know why the father was so happy to see him, don't we? It just supported the unimaginative, self-righteousness of the father and his system. The father was vindicated. He was proven right. The son didn't have the guts to be independent. He had to go sniffling back to good, old, stable Dad. Couldn't stand on his own two feet when the going got tough.

We also know why the brother was so angry and indignant, don't we? He was just more stupid than the father. If he had had a bit more information and intelligence he could have seen that he was being proven right. He was the better of the sons. Furthermore, the younger son would be right back where he wanted him, but even more so than before. Without any money, Daddy's little boy would forever be beholden to his father and older brother, a condition entirely revolting to us free spirits.

Finally, it's easy to see why these religious types like this story. I supports their childish, adolescent ideas of dependence on God: a God which is really a projected father-image. Religious people are really childish people who go scurrying back to their Heavenly Daddy when they get into trouble. They are afraid to stand on their own feet. They tremble before the harsh realities of the world like an adolescent with acne on his first date.

My friends, let us be done with this crutch of religion, this nursery bottle of prayer, this wet nurse of confession, this endless search of a cosmic substitute Father who will take us and cuddle us in his arms like children.

We need men and women who will stand up firmly and bravely in the self-realization of their freedom. The world does not need sobbing, whining adolescents. It needs courageous men and women willing to take the consequences of their actions. It needs men and women who have "come of age."

The Lord's Advocate:

Poor Prodigal Son! Man mountain gone wrong. Hero with an Achilles' heel! If he'd just played it a little differently, he'd have brought it off, wouldn't he?

You made a good try, Devil's Advocate, and you've proved the wrong case. You have defended my case and eloquently. I thank you! Let the congregation be judge and jury.

If your young man had "made it" out there, we might have had to concede. But he didn't make it. He went home to his father, just as you said, even though he had had all the qualifications for being an independent, self-starting, free-spirited, unbound, unconventional cosmopolitan. He had everyone, except.... He had it made, but.... He would have made the grade, if....

Always a condition, always an exception, always a flaw. Yes, he could have done and been all those things *if he had been God*. If he'd had the power, insight, perseverance, wisdom, strength — you name it — of *God*.

But he did not. He was not God. He was a man. And in his heart was an eternal flaw, a fatal flaw, a crack, a cleft in his human will. And that was sin. The willful desire to have everything for himself, to put self at the center of his soul, to let ego reign on the throne of his life.

And every person who has ever lived has always ultimately lost in the battle of life as long as that human flaw was allowed to fester, as long as that crack could remain and widen and deepen into a crevasse, and then a gaping gap: between self and one's humanity, and that one Person and Power who could heal that hole and bridge the breech.

Let's face it: no one makes it on his own. There are no self-made people. We all need someone. And that boy needed his father, and the wonder of that story is that he finally had eyes to see it, and knew it! Jesus' story is to say that that waiting Father, who had let his son go out into the world, was God — the God whom every person who has ever lived needs, and who waits for every one of us to come to our senses, and finally come home to him.

Our national hymn sings: "God mend thine every flaw." And it is faith that finds the flaw in every one of us, and overcomes it.

We all have feet of clay. We all have Samson's hair. We all have Achilles' heels. We all have sin in our souls. That's why we turn tail in life, that's why we crump, why we clam in the clutch, why we boot great opportunities; that's why we so often make a mess of life.

We need God. And that boy knew it. And every person, someday, somehow, ultimately knows it. All of us here know it.

Only God can bridge that gap in our hearts. Only God can throw out that bridge from heaven to earth that provides a safe way across the depths of human sin and failure and evil. And, God has done that for all of us, and for all of history, in the life and death of Jesus Christ. He alone can help us overcome our sin. He alone can give us the hand we need to hold "in making it" on the journey through life. He alone is my hope, and your hope, and the Prodigal Son's hope.

That's the message of the forgiving Father. That's the love that waits for us when we come to our senses. That's the key that alone can make us the strong men and women of the world that your Prodigal was not man enough to be, until he returned to his Father: our Father!

The Great Feast

And the master said to the servant, "Go out to the highways and hedges, and compel people to come in, that my house may be filled. For I tell you, none of these men who were invited shall taste my banquet."

— Luke 14:24

I

The Devil's Advocate:

It's good to be back in your little spiritual ghetto, Mr. Lord's Advocate. It has been a rather busy day for me. I've been visiting a number of churches. Things aren't quite like they used to be. Time was when I could count on most churches to be in my camp. I could usually persuade them to accept some sort of bland, powerless, innocuous liberalism. Or I could get them hung up on a rigid, static fundamentalism. Other churches I could usually mire down in the sludge of national background or the quicksand of an enslaving tradition.

But there are a few churches awakening from their slumber these days, so I'm not able to sleep in on Sunday like I used to. I can't even count on the ski crowd anymore. Would you believe that five or six of your people hurry back from the ski slopes to go to your vesper services? Some people even take their Bibles and other religious books to Florida. It's getting so I can't relax anywhere. I can't depend on people anymore. Some of your Christians are starting to take their religion a little seriously. It's terribly disturbing.

Yet I must say that I do have many, many loyal people who are still on my side. I still have a lot of bloated old fools who huff and puff about their own importance. They, to tell you the truth, are somewhat of a bore. But I have some new, younger types —

vigorous, intelligent young men who are too smart to brag in the usual, obvious ways. Yet if you'll notice carefully, they have subtle means of letting you know that they are nearly the best thing that has happened to America. They think they are making it on their own and won't even acknowledge my power in their lives. Oh, well, who cares about the publicity, so long as I know that I have them in my corner.

And that — Mr. Lord's Advocate — is what your parable is about tonight, isn't it? People in my corner and people in your corner. People who went to your Lord's Feast and people who refused his invitation. Frankly, I think it is a rather embarrassing story for you and your Lord. I should think you would be ashamed to publicize it. After all, it's a story about his failure in society. The people he wanted at his party snubbed him. Consequently, he had to go find some low-class slurpers and sloppers to come to his feast.

You can see it now, can't you? They were poor, dirty, ill-mannered, unkempt, undisciplined, with very little understanding. They were the kind of people who would ask you to pass the "hors de vores" and then drink the finger bowl. They would use the wrong fork, gulp their food, and slurp their coffee. Utterly despicable! Sounds like your Lord had to put his "pearls" out for the swine, since the accepted, respectable, cultured people turned down his invitation.

The Lord's Advocate:

Well, now — faith, and if it isn't Mr. Scratch, Advocate of the Devil, making another attempt at dialoguing out of their "decisions" the people of the Church! I wonder you keep coming back.

And you do have a marvelous imagination. All those boors burping in the banquet hall: it does rather unsettle sensitive suburban stomachs! But really, your penchant for the pungent point has quite run away with you: you've missed the point. My Lord is not left at his banquet with rude, crude, and unattractive rabble whom he didn't want. He's always had his own people; and they always have been little people: unassuming, honest, humble, little people.

"Little" in the sense of lowly, in heart. "Little" in the sense of letting the blustering blow-hards babble on, and toot their own horns without feeling insecure and having to get in on the social and spiritual gamesmanship gag.

This is a parable about the people who've been yours from the beginning: the people who've been hanging around the church for years, maybe, but just "playing" at "church." It's about those pompous, parading, professional religionists who were sitting around at the Chief Pharisee's house one of the days Jesus was invited for dinner. He saw them all jockeying for position, taking the best seats at the table, elbowing each other out, gesturing, snubbing, playing the "Do you know who" game and generally being snobs and bores.

He had just been telling them a real dinner party ought to be for those who cannot pay you back.

The Kingdom of God, he was saying, is like a great feast that God gives. He knows who his real friends are, who is really indebted to him and grateful to him, but can't really do anything to pay him back: the ordinary sinners of the world whom the rich and religiously superficial look down upon.

The slobby, snobby ones he invited because he's always ready to give them a chance.

But, as you say, they already are yours, many of them, and they really can't be bothered to make the effort to go and sit down with their Lord in the Kingdom. They have a thousand excuses.

They never were his. You've already identified the Lord's own. They're the ones, as you say, who'll read a Bible in Florida, or give up an hour's skiing for vespers, or make 101 other sacrifices to put Christ first, where they want him in their lives.

And you'd better be busy, Mr. Scratch: you'd better get to church these Sundays and feed 'em the old line — like, "You don't want to listen to this stuff; this is boring, old-fashioned, uninteresting." Because you're losing, man! Look at 'em out there — the troops of the Lord. Catch 'em if you can.

II

The Devil's Advocate:

Of course, Mr. Lord's Advocate, you will try to twist this story to your advantage. But it seems to me it will take some doing. Because in every case, the very people whom you would most want to have at a party, wouldn't come. They all sent their "regrets" to your Lord, which is to say, they weren't too impressed with him.

Take the first man, for instance. He turned down the invitation because he had bought some real estate — a field — and he had to go out to see it. A perfectly legitimate reason for not accepting an invitation to the party, if you ask me. After all, what is more important than the world of business? Your Lord was a terribly impractical and demanding type of person anyway. He would say such things as, "Unless you give up houses and lands and even family, for my sake, you can have no part of me."

Now I ask you, isn't that absurd? Doesn't all that sound like the demands of a wild-eyed fanatic? Your Lord was a kooky radical! He may not have been the Messiah, but he certainly had the Messiah complex. Such outrageous demands.

Well, my man who went to look after his real estate saw through all that fanaticism. He was not going to get hooked on your Lord's unrealistic requirements. He knew what was important in life. So he was not going to waste his precious time associating with your Lord. He could do that in any off moment.

My man had a motto — "First things first" — and that meant "property before parties," and "property before religion." My disciples and I know what really counts in the world. Property counts. It comes way ahead of religion. Look at your own people gathered here (if they really are yours). Most of them would never think of letting their property run down. They keep it in constant repair and freshly painted. Their lawns are a lush, velvet green, manicured like the White House gardens. Their cars and offices are resplendent examples of efficiency, beauty, and thoughtful attention. Yet, Mr. Opponent, it really amuses me to see how little time they spend improving their religion. I really have to laugh to see how hard you have to work to get your troops out on Sunday morning. And

Sunday evening is even more of a joke. Sometimes I wonder if it is even worth my effort on Sunday nights. Yet I must say I delight in your embarrassment of your troop's poor showing.

You'd better give in, Mr. Lord's Advocate. Your people, as well as mine, believe that property is more important than religion.

The Lord's Advocate:

Give in? Why should I? My Lord's lads don't put property above religion. The man with the excuse about real estate was just one of the types the Lord found in the Pharisee's house when he was telling this parable.

He could see them all around him: the money-men, the men with holdings — property, house in city and country, stocks and bonds, insurance — all the man-made supports and shoring-ups. Like the rich young man, they didn't have their hearts with him and he could see it. They weren't fooling anyone. Least of all, Jesus of Nazareth! He knew just where he stood with them. And he knew they'd do him in the second it was ever a choice between him and their bank rolls and beautiful lawns. He knew they weren't interested in his feast, his Kingdom.

Because the Jesus-gang are the guys who decided right at the beginning who they belonged to, and where they were going. They might have property, and money too. He wasn't against their being rich. They just hadn't sold their souls to it. They weren't so insecure that they had to use money and property as a crutch, as a defense for their timid egos, or as a defense against all those threatening movements of society that looked as though they might make them think, and pray, and wrestle with their consciences, and maybe give up something.

Not at all. They are the ones who are sharing what they have with Christ. They are the ones who are giving generously to the Christian cause, who believe in — home and foreign missions — and are supporting both, liberally. They are the ones who believe people of other races and religions are their brothers and sisters and have a right to live anywhere they can afford — and are welcoming them from the city to suburbia, and are selling houses to them, and inviting them out from the city to dinner, and are having African-Americans for summer preachers in their churches, and are eager and glad to have all kinds of races and backgrounds in upscale suburbs! Heavens! They are so safe and secure in the Lord, and so unthreatened by contemporary social pressures to change, that they think intermarriage between different races and religions for their daughters and sons, or anybody else's, should be perfectly acceptable — providing the young people love each other and love the Lord.

It's your boys — even when they have sneaked in and infiltrated the ranks of the church — who are the race-baiters, and the restrictive covenant, gentleman's agreement signers, and the property protectors, who are so insecure and unbelieving that they storm out of church, or school, or club, or neighborhood with a big man-on flourish, when they are threatened. The property-poops are yours, Mr. Devil's Advocate. You might as well claim them!

III

The Devil's Advocate:

I must say, Mr. Lord's Advocate, that sometimes I almost feel sorry for you. My troops outnumber yours fantastically, and I have all the people that really count. Take, for instance, the next fellow in the parable who refused your Lord's invitation. He had purchased five yoke of oxen and had to go see about them. Of course, that doesn't sound like much to us, but in his day that many oxen represented power.

You get the point, don't you? The man turned down your Lord for power. He decided he wasn't going to run around with a lot of anemic, innocuous religious ideas. Those things come and go like fads and fancies. He knew that most religious feeling is whimsical. It isn't stable or strong. It's here today, gone tomorrow.

But as for power — it will always be around. That's what men went for in the day of our parable, and it's what they go for today. Even your people know there's no power in the Church. I note, for example, that most of your parents would be aghast if one of their fine sons should choose the ministry. Just the other day I heard a delightful story of a family like that. The father, in this case, was quite well-to-do. He had been active in the church all his life, and was considered to be one of the "pillars." He even gave ten percent of his income to the church — and in his case, ten percent was quite a lot.

Then one day his number one son came home and announced, "Dad, I've decided to enter the ministry." There was a sudden, deathly silence — something like the calm before the tornado. Sure enough, there was a tornado coming. Finally, his exasperated, pillar-of-the-church dad exploded in all directions at once. "What?!" he exclaimed. "Go into the ministry? Are you out of your mind? Don't be so stupid! Do something worthwhile with your life. The ministry has neither power nor money."

At last report, the son was in a state of shock and the father had gone to Florida for his heart condition.

There you have it, the true story of a very wise father and a very stupid son. Fathers who really know the score don't want their sons messing around with religion, except maybe as an extracurricular activity. They want them going after the power and the money. The Church has neither one of them. Neither does your Lord. That's why the man long ago turned down the religious invitation to look after his power interests. And that's the reason sensible fathers do not want their sons in a religious vocation today.

The Lord's Advocate:

No power in the Church, eh? You really think that's why the man with a stable full of oxen or a stable full of autos would explode when his son announced for the ministry?

For one thing, he's only another one of your false-front, stuffed-shirt interlopers on the Church scene. That kind has always been yours, Mr. Devil — the sort who does everything right on the surface, even down to the ten percent of income to the Lord: on top of loud talk about morality, and marijuana, and the terrible younger generation, and the society going to the dogs. He's no more a soldier of the Lord committed to battle than a ten-year-old playing war with a broomstick!

The real reason he explodes at his son's decision is that he sees his son going over to the other side. It's the Church, he suspects, and all those radical leaders from Jesus down to his own parish minister who really are the ones stirring up all the trouble in society today. They're the ones making people restless, making them look beneath the surface of things, and seeing the subtleties of the human spirit, and the insinuations of selfishness, and hate, and anger, and brutality, and prejudice, and have fed a whole new philosophy to a generation of students, and have gotten the whole society up in arms and marching for justice, honor, and truth.

"Onward, Christian soldiers, marching as to war,
With the Cross of Jesus going on before."

That's war with him, and he knows a lot of things he subtly supports are going to burn — and he can't stand that! The ministry, naturally, is the last thing he wants his son doing.

Because the ministry in the Christian Church, whether by laymen or ordained professionals, is more and more where the power is these days. Look at Martin Luther King! Look at Pope John. Or Peter Marshall. Or Billy Graham. None of that! They're too much. Too much power. Too much dynamite: because that's the power, from the cross and crown of Jesus Christ, that changes minds and wins hearts, and turns the world upside down.

IV

The Devil's Advocate:

Well, Mr. Lord's Advocate, your arguments are very interesting. I'm sure there are lots of people who would like to believe you, but who know that in the face of the world's realities, they cannot.

Notice that the third man in the parable who refused your Lord's invitation was also a good, solid, stable type — he was a family man. He had married a wife and had entered into the delights of sex and the responsibilities of home and family. I think that even you, Mr. Lord's Advocate, would be pleased to know that this man was not a sex dilettante. He was a responsible type. He just knew what came first — the wife and family.

Of course, I notice that even among your people the family does not come first. Business or profession is usually first. School and clubs compete for second place. Family is probably third or fourth. Church and religious activities, however, are way down the line in priority. And that, of course, is the way it should be.

If money and power do not form the center of a man's life, pleasure certainly should, and sexual pleasure surely will. Families are important, too. We need them to keep our system of power and economics going. As for churches and your Lord — they make very little difference.

Smart men, men-in-the-know, are aware of all this, so that's why they declined your Lord's invitation. They knew he didn't know the score. That's why your Lord had to go into the slums and boondocks to get people to come. He attracted the ignorant, the powerless, the crude, uncultured types. They were the bums, the dropouts, the ne'er-do-wells. But the enlightened men of property, power, and pleasure declined the invitation. They knew they didn't need your Lord. He had nothing to give them.

The Lord's Advocate:

There, you're right. He had much to give them: but what many of them did not want. The people who have suffered and sinned in life are very likely to be the ones who know their humanity, and that they need the Lord. They've grown beyond pomposity and fake-out religion. They know life the way it is — and they come from all sections of society to the Lord's Great Feast. Nobody has to beg them to come. They know it's their dish, their need. And their hearts — many of them — have already found the Lord.

But your family man is just another of those frauds Jesus saw all about him. He probably had heard, as I have, the old family excuse: "Sorry, Reverend, we can't come to church, because we're so busy being a good family, going off on trips and weekends together, eating late Sunday morning breakfast at home, together — you know — that sort of thing!"

Families have a wonderful excuse. They're the excuse for cutting somebody else up in business, striving to get ahead, beating someone else out for a sale, working late for the company, wearing yourself out for the corporation — "Gotta do it for the wife and kids! Gotta support them in a decent style. Need to earn for their education."

Oh, yes — but none of what that family really needs! No prayer, no Bible, no church, no faith! Great!

No — Jesus said — you've got to put me first — even before families and friends and money and that whole bit. And if you do it for my sake and the gospel's — if you dare to lose your life — you'll find it in a more abundant way than ever before!

The church is here to help 'em see that any man can really do this — can really give his life away for Jesus. And my Lord dares us all here tonight to run that risk, and take that chance, and find the real power, the real excitement, the real fun, the real joy that makes life count.

That's the feast, the banquet, the kingdom which Christ is offering us!

The Ten Virgins

... And those who were ready went in with him to the marriage feast. Afterward other maidens came also, saying, "Lord, Lord, open to us." But he replied, "... I do not know you." Watch therefore, for you know neither the day nor the hour. — Matthew 25:10-13

I

The Devil's Advocate:

The story of the ten virgins is a delightful little piece from the quaint past of a tiny and quaint country. It purports to be full of the happy joy of a wedding day and the festive mood of the well-wishing crowd. And the ten virgins had the task of keeping the bride company while she awaited the bridegroom's coming. Since he usually came unexpectedly at night, it was their task to keep their lamps in readiness to light the way for him. It was quite a delightful custom.

But I have changed all that, along with the help of my disciples. In the first place, in today's world, look at the difficulty you would have finding ten girls who would qualify as virgins. With the modern sex codes which have been introduced, most girls wouldn't be caught dead as a virgin on *their* wedding day or anybody else's. Whoever would want to be so naïve, so innocent and inexperienced? Not our modern girls. You'll never find them dancing around, giggly-like, on a wedding day. Listen, they know the score. The only reason most of their friends get married is because they get pregnant.

Giggly virgins at weddings are a thing of the past. My girls are much more knowledgeable, blasé, and realistic — they know that the only real enjoyment of sex is outside of marriage. It's only the suckers and weak-hearted who get trapped into marriage.

The Lord's Advocate:

Well, looks like the secretaries were right! The dialogue this time is going to be a juicy one! Guess we just have to have a little prologue about sex before we can get into the meaning of the Parable of the Ten Virgins. With the University of Minnesota achieving new fame lately with courses like "Sex For Credit," I suppose we could bill this as "Sunday Night Sex," or possibly something reassuring like, "Always On Sunday."

Of course, that's really no joke. Maybe what America needs is a lot more sex on Sunday — a lot more teaching about sex by the Christian Church, and a lot more recognition by everyone that what you are on Sunday, what you hear, and say, and believe on Sunday had better jolly well begin to have something to do with how we live our sexual lives on Monday, Tuesday, and Wednesday.

Until we get God into our view of sex, we won't see that the only free, open, loving, happy, really "sexy" sex is the secure, safe, relaxed relationship that is possible in the intimacy and commitment of marriage. The intercourse indulged in the parked car, the college dormitory, or the motel room by the high school or college students who say, "It's okay because we love each other and have a meaningful relationship," can never be more than a pitiful imitation of the free, happy, loving act that can take place when you've publicly promised your life, your love, your support, and your faithfulness to a partner in marriage.

A lot of girls and a lot of guys don't understand this. A lot of Christian girls and Christian guys don't understand this. And there are fewer virgins at the altar today when weddings come.

Whose fault is it? God knows. Mine, I think, and yours. Let's let sex be something sacred. Let's give it a chance, again. Let's let women be people again, and not things. Let's get them off of billboards, and out of automobile advertising, and out of all the tawdry trade made of them.

You businessmen do it, and you advertising men, you publishers, and you parents, and we preachers! The tragedy of only ten virgins, when there ought to be 100, is a tragedy of our time.

The Devil's Advocate sees well into our sinful hearts. Let us take heed!

II

The Devil's Advocate:

The main point of this parable is not about virgins or the lack of them and, of course, it's not about weddings either. Rather, as we know, it is about being ready for the bridegroom when he comes. And, of course, the early Christians understood Jesus to be the bridegroom who was going to come again for his bride, the Church. Consequently, this parable is to teach Christians to be prepared for the second coming of Christ. Christians are supposed to be like the five wise virgins who had enough oil in their lamps. They were prepared to wait for a long time for Christ's coming whereas the five foolish virgins were not prepared for a long wait.

It is, of course, a charming story, but it is irrelevant and unheeded. People have wised up. They have seen that Jesus didn't come through with his promises. Most of the early Christians believed he was coming again in power and glory during their lifetime. Even Paul, the apostle, believed that. Yet that same Paul had to begin to alter his beliefs during his lifetime. He began to admit that Jesus was delaying his coming.

And he was not the only one. Christians throughout the Church began to wonder where their Lord was. Many of them looked longingly into the sky for him, only to be disappointed day after day right up to their graves. "When is he coming?" they would ask. And others would answer, "Remember that with the Lord a day is as a thousand years and a thousand years a day." So they put off in their questioning and they went down to their graves with a big question mark. Where was Jesus?

And that's what Christians have been asking for centuries. "Where is Jesus? Where is Jesus in all his power and glory as he promised?" So in all countries of the world, among old people and young, you'll find upturned faces scanning the skies for his coming.

And when they've finished scanning, they lie down and die like everyone else. He didn't come. Yes, they had to face life's ultimate reality before they realized he wasn't coming. In a way it's sad that people can follow such delusions so long with so much hope. But on the other hand, I say it serves them right, trying to follow such a pipe dream.

The Lord's Advocate:

Pipe dream, you say? Not at all. They hope and we hope for Christ's coming in the clouds of glory — not at all as an impossible dream, but as a daily-authenticated assurance!

"Why?" you say. Why can we persist in holding such hope? Because for us, Jesus has already come again! Not in visible public power and glory — but in the just as real unseen power of his Holy Spirit! He rose in the Resurrection with a body his disciples saw. He moved among them, appeared to them all. And he told them exactly what would happen: "I will pray the Father, and he shall send you the Holy Spirit. The Holy Spirit who will come to you in my name, he shall bring all things to your remembrance, whatsoever I have said unto you." And then he said, "Lo, I am with you always — even unto the end of the world!" And this word: "Wait in Jerusalem until you have been endowed with power from on high."

He's with us right now. We have life. He lives! He's alive and at work — in his Church throughout the world. Don't you believe "Christ is dead, and long live the Devil until he comes again!" He'll come all right, in visible glory. But we don't have to worry and wait. He'll come when he's ready. He'll come when the world can't stand not knowing him another minute. He'll come when every knee in heaven and on earth shall bow to him, and the Kingdom of God is ready and waiting to come in the heart of every person alive.

But we — we live in the age of the Holy Spirit. This tremendous time when our Christ moves like wind through the world — touching down everywhere where people claim him, in persons.

Maybe the parable of the ten virgins is not about sitting around and waiting for the Second Coming. Maybe it's about a fickle Church of Jesus Christ who knows the Lord is coming some day, some time, and still doesn't prepare itself to receive Jesus. Maybe it's about people like you and me, who have been invited to come to the Great Marriage Feast of the Church and the Lord, but forfeit our chance to be there because we don't care enough to get ready: enough to prepare the lamp of our lives to burn bright for him.

Maybe it's told for people who refuse to sing, "This little light of mine — I'm gonna let it shine!"

We'll never have it shining in us unless we prepare the wick with the oil of a daily walk with Christ: a daily prayer life with Jesus. A daily reading of the Word. A daily living, witnessing, shining, life of preparation for every day, as if it were the Kingdom-day.

III

The Devil's Advocate:

I am delighted to see, however, that most of you no longer believe in Christ's second coming. After all, just think of the oil you would have burned up standing around with those virgins for twenty centuries. Most of you have given up on that nonsense. You know he isn't coming. He has left you stranded.

But I notice that you have learned how to make the best of it. You get so you feel very much at home in this world. So you really don't look forward to another one very seriously. And I'm with you. You're makin' it right here and now. You are a people come of age. You are a secular people of the secular city. With soft carpets and climate-controlled homes and cars, who needs heaven? This is the good life. As for heaven or the second coming of Christ, who knows when that will be, if ever?

Just think how many people there have been throughout the centuries who have dolled themselves up in white robes to stand on mountaintops to wait for the Lord. Now I ask you, how do you face your friends after a fiasco like that? That's why it pays not to be an excitable type. People who believe in the Lord's return are perpetually disappointed. That's why it's better to forget all that and "make it" here and now.

Have you noticed how severe and austere those other-worldly types are? They look at you out of those sad, solemn eyes as if you're going to hell unless you become as somber as they. There's not a Good Time Charlie among them. They're all Bad Time Henriettas.

Besides, the people who really do something about life here and now are those who have given up a second coming and hereafter. They have learned it's no use whining to the sky hoping Jesus will come and make it better. You have to do it yourself. After all, that's the American way. We are practical people who get things done. We have made the Kingdom of God come on earth in our time. It's not in the future. It's here, by the power of our hands.

The Lord's Advocate:

Oh, yes, we are practical people. But what most Americans are building is not the Kingdom of God. That's hardly what we're building in wars or in the central cities, or on the college campuses. We are building a military machine the horror of whose might is beyond our imagining. In the cities we are building a divided city of haves and have-nots, a situation for revolution. And on the campuses we are teaching glorification of man and his might and pompous arrogance that is repelling a whole generation of students — and should repel us!

Oh, no — the people who are doing something creative and constructive about life here are precisely the people who have settled it in their hearts once and for all that Jesus is their Lord and liege, that to his Kingdom they give their commitment forever, and, trusting in that Christ who, on the cross, loved and saved them, claim heaven as their heritage, and have given all to the One who is victorious over death and so have paved the way to life beyond death for them!

When you've settled that and are no longer terrorized by the threat of death — then you are the one who is free to live life now, freely and wholly and completely and victoriously!

So — the Christians are the swingers! They're the ones who are living it up. Living it up with love, and laughter, and loyal service to their Lord.

They're happy. They are making it — because Christ is coming, and they're going to heaven.

IV

The Devil's Advocate:

The last thing to say about this parable is that it's unfair. Look who is criticized — the five virgins who ran out of oil. And as they run off to buy some, the bridegroom comes and then he refuses to let the gals into the wedding party when they return with their oil. He closes the door against them and claims he never knew them, which was a lie. He knew who they were. They had been waiting for him for hours so they could honor him. Anyone can see that they received lousy treatment.

Yet this parable is supposed to illustrate the coming of Jesus. Sunday after Sunday my opponent assures us that Jesus is loving and compassionate, slow to anger, merciful and quick to forgive. If that is the case, why does he shut out those five virgins who've been standing around waiting for him? Where is all his forgiveness and kindness and mercy? At least they were trying. At least they were looking for him. They weren't even out partying it up. Kind of makes you wonder, doesn't it? You wonder if it's worthwhile to wait for him, don't you?

Listen, if he's waited twenty centuries to come, you can be sure he'll wait twenty more. Who knows if he exists? No one really knows. So eat, drink, and be merry, for tomorrow you may die and the good life will have passed you by.

I'll let you in on one more little secret. These religious types believe the same way I do. But they've got a thing going. They know that they can make money off you if you fear Christ's coming again and his threat of judgment. They try to convince you that you are all louses so you'll feel guilty and be afraid of judgment. And once you are guilty and afraid of judgment they know you will come to church, give your money, and even serve on a church committee as an act of penance.

So you see, my friends, it's a high-class, well-organized swindle based on your guilt feelings and your fear of judgment. Do you think these religious Joes really care about you? They care only about themselves, about their image and prestige. They're not concerned about how you look before God, but how they look before their peers and denominational officials. You are no more than a customer for their religious businesses. To put it rather indelicately, my friends, you are suckers.

Of course, it grieves me to say all this so bluntly, but I want you to know that I am your friend. I am attempting to save you from delusion and false hopes. I want you to see that your guilt feelings are being exploited by ecclesiastical egos. Your fear of judgment is being used for a handsome profit. Look how the clergy have exploited poor and rich in claiming control over their sojourn in the afterlife.

It's all a hoax. Don't hang around the church with false hopes. Use your oil for a good time. Christ isn't coming again.

The Lord's Advocate:

Want to bet? We can wait as long as you can. We can wait longer. Because the Lord who is someday coming, has given us work to do now — exciting, important, lifesaving work.

And nobody's deluding us. We could "eat, drink, and be merry" if we wanted. Our way is more fun, that's all. Look what we have: the best friends a person could ask for, the love of tremendous people, and the chance to tell the world the best news it has ever heard! We have lots to do — a busy harvest to gather in before he comes.

The chaps who can't be bothered with heeding the message, and getting ready for Christ, and praying, and studying the scripture, and worshiping with the church, and learning and serving, are not being turned away from the love and joy of the bridegroom. They're shutting themselves out. They are refusing to pay the price — love's price.

But it's not too late. They can turn and repent. They can take up their cross, and deny themselves, and join the band of brothers and sisters who work and wait with joy for Jesus. You come too!

The Unprofitable Servant

Now after a long time the master of those servants came and settled accounts ... To the first two servants he said, "Well done, good and faithful servants you have been faithful over a little, I will set you over much." But to the third servant he said, "You wicked and slothful servant...."
— Matthew 25:19, 21, 26

I

The Devil's Advocate:

My dear friends, I consider it a great privilege to be able to address you on a topic very close to your heart and mine — the topic of money and its use. Indeed, it is more than the topic of money — it is the topic of life itself, and how we should use it. I feel that it is a privilege to address you because I think many of you will be on my side. Heretofore, it has been my opinion that my opponent, The Lord's Advocate, has had the distinct advantage. It is to be remembered that I am having to make my case on his territory, right in the midst of his people.

Yet, I take particular delight in being able to address you because I am confident that many of you interpret this parable of the talents the same way as I interpret it. And quite frankly, nothing could delight me more than to see the Lord's Advocate embarrassed before his own troops.

You should be warned that he will attempt to exhort you to all sorts of foolish excesses. He will raise wild-eyed arguments and unprovable opinions. He will appeal to your romantic notions and sense of adventure. Note well the assault he will make on your calm reasonableness and your cool assessment of hard reality. So please allow me to forewarn you. I have your interests very much at heart, even if I have been given a rather unfortunate name. But do not let that deter you. Let me assure you that I have huge numbers of people who regularly argue for, believe in, and live out my position.

Of course, the majority of them are not in church. They are out for dinner or watching television or enjoying some other sort of diversion. Ah, yes, they are all mine. I love them. They know it's useless to bother with church. They already believe in my arguments.

But, of course, I am always glad to have the opportunity to do some recruiting. How wonderful it is! It is so deceitful and delightful because I can read your minds and hearts and I know some of you are secretly on my side already. Even though you are here, you wish you weren't. A perfectly marvelous attitude. So deceitful! Ah, well, it is his turn, so think about the television programs you will be watching when you get home.

The Lord's Advocate:

Well, I am glad to be here, too — with the people who certainly should achieve the annual "we try harder" trophy, for effort.

Maybe you think you have the money-mad here tonight, Mr. Scratch, but you're so interested in the green stuff yourself that you may have misjudged the majority. I won't deny they're missing something on television. But maybe they'll really get it here tonight, much more than they might get at home. In fact, this may be a bigger boon right here.

And maybe they know it! Maybe that's why they're here. Because these types already suspect that the real values of life are not in color television or green-colored paper or any of the things they can buy. You may not find us so hung up over money as you think! Take it from here, friend!

II

The Devil's Advocate:

I would like to take the opportunity to point out a few facts about this parable. Notice first of all how unfair this fellow was. He didn't treat his employees the same. All men are created equal, you know. Yet he gave one man $5,000, the other $2,000, and the third only $1,000. Now I ask you, is that fair? Is he giving each man equal opportunity? Certainly not.

Yet I have heard my idealistic opponent fulminate regularly Sunday after Sunday that all men are created equal and that all men should be given equal opportunity. But look. Right here in one of Jesus' teachings you have preferential treatment. Some people are getting the advantage. Any idiot knows it's better to have $5,000 to invest rather than $1,000. You can do so much more with it. You have more freedom and confidence.

Let me point out another fact of this parable that is much overlooked. Note what the employer says to the employee who received only $1,000. "You wicked and slothful servant! You knew that I reap where I have not sowed and gather where I have not winnowed." Did you get that? The employer even admits that he is a hard and rapacious man. He'll grab whatever he can get wherever and whenever he has the opportunity. It doesn't bother him to muscle in on somebody else. So long as he can do it without too much resistance, he will. If a guy is sucker enough not to have the proper protection on his fortune, this fellow in Jesus' parable will abscond with it. He is an extortioner, a wheeler-dealer with no scruples, save one. And that is — make money as fast as you can, any way that you can.

So you see who is criticized in this parable. It is the man who has scruples. Just imagine the methods used by those other two fellows who doubled their investment in the time their employer was away. Yet Jesus praises them and condemns the fellow who didn't invest his $1,000.

This leads me to mention the final fact about this story of unspeakable injustice. The $1,000 was taken away from the third man and given to the man who had been given $5,000. And since that man had doubled his investment he would now have a total of $11,000! I ask you, have you ever heard of such outrageous injustice? Yet Jesus uses this story.

So now let us see how our devious opponent will attempt to spin some sort of innocuous truth out of this one.

The Lord's Advocate:

Nothing devious — just a question: Was he really so unjust? So unfair that one received $5,000 and another $2,000 and the third only $1,000? Indeed, all men are created equal: equal in every opportunity they need to make meaning out of life, equal in God's sight as his children to be loved.

But not all the same. Not all good, not all equal in ability, brain, and motivation. And the scripture says that the man of wealth divided his money among his servants "in proportion to their abilities." One of them deserved, by proven initiative and faithfulness, to be entrusted with $5,000. The man given $1,000 had measured up to no more risk than that.

And yet, he was not counted out. He was given a chance. He could prove himself with the little if he had the will, the daring, the faith.

And isn't that, after all, the key? Jesus told the story saying, "The Kingdom of God is like one man receiving $5,000 and another $2,000 and another $1,000. The Kingdom of God is a gift, an opportunity. And the man with a $5,000 faith is given a $5,000 opportunity." Each of us, the Lord was saying, is given a chance for great adventure with God. Every day the opportunity comes. It's come to us. It is coming to us tonight. Do we take it? That's what Jesus wants to know. That's what the story is about: about what we do with the Kingdom when it is handed to us.

Some grasp it as a golden chance: they use it, they let their light shine before men, they tell the world about their Christ, they "spread the blessing." And their $5,000 of faith becomes $10,000. And so with the $2,000 man with less.

But the man with the $1,000 faith really doesn't have the spirit. He is without the daring. Really without the trust — and he immediately resorts to rationalization, to excuses for not doing anything with his faith-opportunity. All he does is blame God for not having given him more. He buries his chances. He doesn't bother to pray, to read the Bible, to know God. He does nothing. And he receives nothing. His faith is no greater when he's through.

But worse still, the kingdom is no greater. It has gained sway over no more lives under this man's hand. It has not been extended.

And instead of simply not doing good, not making money, not increasing the world's faith, he has lost ground for the Kingdom. He has retreated, shrunk the reaches of his Lord's domain. He is an unprofitable servant and *deserves* to have taken away from him even what he had.

Harsh judgment perhaps, by the world's standards — which are static. But by God's standards, which are dynamic and growing, he had lost the battle. He was defeated. And so he was plundered, and deserved to be. Complete fair play in the game God plays!

III

The Devil's Advocate:

Contrary to the misguided opinions of our opponent, the man who buried his money was pretty smart. Those fellows who invested were just lucky. What if there had been a recession in the market? What if there had been a depression? What if their President had slowed down the market by increasing interest rates? What if they had bought a bad stock at a bad time? What if the bottom had fallen out of the economy? Where would those $2,000 and $5,000 fellows be now? They would be broke and in the soup and bread line. And just think how many people would have liked to go out in their backyard to dig up a buried treasure of $1,000. That would be better in the long run than watching it sink into oblivion with the stock market.

Of course, we all know who Jesus was attacking. It was the scribes and Pharisees and other leaders of legalistic Judaism. He was angry at them for resisting his new teachings about religion. He claimed they were clutching their laws and rituals and religious teachings like the man clutched his $1,000. So he criticizes them for being so narrow and conservative. He wants them to be reckless and foolish by investing themselves in his religion. Jesus was reacting to opposition.

But I ask you, why should they change? Why should they give up a religion that had been with them over 1,300 years? It had taken nearly 900 years for their religious teachings and traditions to develop. They had beautiful worship facilities in the Temple in Jerusalem and in the synagogues throughout Palestine.

Of course, it is true that many of the more radical and fanatic types believed that a new messiah or king was coming. But there was certainly no reason to believe that Jesus was the one. After all, look where he came from — Nazareth of Galilee. What a despicable place! You might as well say he came from the hills of Tennessee or the prairies of the Dakotas! Nothing good can come from those places.

Besides, Jesus had the audacity to call those dear, devoted, religious men — the Pharisees — he had the audacity to call them sons-of-the-devil (a curious compliment, I must say), painted graves full of dead men's bones. How could he do that? These men had been in religious circles all their lives. They had been in Inter-Varsity Christian Fellowship, Campus Crusade for Christ, and the United Christian Campus Fellowship while in college. They had been active in seminary activities and received their Master of Divinity, the professional ministerial degree. Moreover, many had gone on to graduate school both at home and abroad and had received both master's and doctor's degrees. They were highly qualified.

One time when a farmer came to visit them, he asked the Doctors of Religion if God in fact loved man and cared about him. They pointed out that it depends a great deal on how you define God, love, and man. If you define God as the self-projected image of wish fulfillment, then "God" does indeed love man unless, of course, you define man as essentially self-hating because of guilt feelings aroused by society's demands upon man, demands which are idealized into absolute standards and reinforced by the concept of "God" who supports these standards. Of course, it was a little difficult for the farmer to grasp all that the first time around. So they advised him to read the complete works of Freud, Nietzsche, and Marx, along with those of Kierkegaard, Barth, Tillich, and Niebuhr.

A thoroughly efficient answer, wouldn't you say? Did they give him any foolish, simple-minded answer? Not at all! Did they delude him into thinking that religion was an easy thing, something you could get overnight? Not these boys! They were professionals from the word go. They were not going around spouting off easy answers to complex questions.

So how could they get excited about Jesus of Nazareth? Where had he gone to school? Who were his teachers? Where did he come from? His family was blue-collar class. He had published nothing in the leading professional journals. There were no books under his name. Most all the professional religious types knew nothing about him except that they violently disagreed with him.

So you see, they were protecting what they had. They were not going to risk their $1,000 of religion on something new and untried. Moses, Abraham, and the prophets they knew. But for this man Jesus, they neither knew from whence he had come or where he was going. So why risk their whole past on him?

The Lord's Advocate:

And it was a risk, you're right. Venture capital, it was, with a man's own heart — and any one of us would do well to think twice before laying it on the line with an unknown like the Nazarene. The scribes and Pharisees were cautious, and they should be!

But how cautious? And for how long? If Jesus of Nazareth was God's man of the hour, bringing God's Kingdom in power, then the wise man is not only the cautious man. He's the man who has eyes to see and ears to hear! The man who can see the signs of the time, who can tell when history's hour has struck.

And you have the issue right: it was the time either to bury what you had and hang on in apprehensive hope, or to cast care to the wind, and "go big" in faith for a long-term, no hesitation investment! And the capital they were concerned with was faith.

And you are right — the scribes and Pharisees did have something to defend: a long and great tradition, a good tradition, which had been precious to Abraham, Isaac, and Jacob. Not something you set aside in a moment! They could indeed have watched everything they cared about washed away forever with this Jesus if the risk was wrong and he was no Christ.

And, of course, his only proof was himself: the life he lived, the truth he taught, the love he gave, and finally the death he died. But, of course, they didn't really look at that, did they? They cast about for credentials. They made the mistake of religious men in every century: they judged by external appearances, by institutional forms, by predetermined procedures.

And by those standards, Jesus was a washout! Nazareth was nowhere! East Nothingsville! And isn't it strange what we take as standards — college, seminary, proper ordination, official blessing from the right circles, getting published in the right journals, having your books widely acclaimed.

Jesus had none of these. All he had was himself: his heart, his hand, his hope to offer man. And, he had God.

A tough choice — God or the right graduate degrees. And isn't it sad the scribes and Pharisees chose the degrees and not God. We sympathize with them. But they were wrong. They did miss their chance. And the whole people of Israel missed their chance because these men were wrong, because they didn't see, because they were blind. They gambled — as they had every right to do — and they lost. It is one of the tragedies of the ages!

The only tragedy greater will be if we too are blind and do not have eyes to see that this man, in spite of coming from Nazareth, and having no academic credentials, is Christ the Lord, Son of God, and our Savior.

IV

The Devil's Advocate:

Let me remind you of what I said at the very beginning — my opponent will try to allure you by false promises and emotional exhortations to adventure which can only lead to oblivion. Let me again appeal to your cool head, your balanced judgment, your hard reasonableness.

The first thing to remember is that you have to look skeptically at all religious reformers. Look at all these fly-by-night evangelists — the Elmer Gantrys, the snake-handlers, the bright-eyed, innocent Campus Crusaders who have a simplistic answer to all the world's problems. They are like the souped-up, "Jesus-is-the-big-shot's-buddy" Christianity of Young Life. Campus Crusade and all the assorted self-appointed Bible teachers claim, "Jesus is the answer." But as one college sophomore put it, "What is the question?"

So I ask you, why not hold on to the religious instruction which you already have? Why abandon the professionals? Half these religious reformers running around are money-grabbing egomaniacs. They want you to give your heart to Jesus but your pocketbook to them. So why shouldn't you protect your $1,000 worth of religious treasure? Why should you throw it overboard for something unproven and untried? Why take a chance? Hang on to that which you have.

After all, that is the practice of religious denominations. Do you think they would give up what they have to go after something new? It is not very likely. Since Lutheranism is working for the Scandinavians and assorted Germans, why should they rethink it or abandon it for something else? Since Presbyterianism works for the Scotch, Catholicism for the Latins and Irish, and Anglicanism for the English, why risk all that for something new?

Since the Dutch liked to be Reformed, and
Since the Baptists like to be reborn, and

Since the Methodists like the Anglican outcaste, and
Since the Quakers like quietly to resist the draft, and

Since the Christian Scientists the doctors fear, and
Since the Congregationalists keep saying loud and clear,

"Remember the Mayflower," until they are small enough to get back on it, and

Since denominations, confident of their doctrine may not be,
You can be quite sure, they'd never give up bureaucracy.

So if religious leaders and denominations won't risk their old religious ideas on the new, why should you? I say, hide your religious convictions deep in your heart — bury them there. Preserve them. Don't let anyone get at them. All this wild-eyed investing in novel religious ideas will cease. People who cast about so foolishly will only get foolish answers.

The scribes and Pharisees were right. They protected their investment. They held on to what they had. They were not deluded by the claims of Jesus. And I am sure that cool, conservative people such as yourselves will not be deluded either.

The Lord's Advocate:

I hope they will not be deluded. I hope they will protect their investment. What Christ wants to know is what is their investment? Is it in the past, in tradition, in custom, in denominations and their narrowed views, and their increasingly anachronistic bureaucracies — or, is it in him, in Jesus Christ, the Son of Man, and Son of God?

I admit that a man who is trying to present Christ to the world does oversimplify. Sin is every man's sorrow, and it's the Christian's too. The glassy-eyed, spiritual scalp-takers who are only interested in adding up conversions are a distortion of true discipleship just as much as the denominational bureaucrats, and the professors in the theological cemeteries, and the silk-gowned establishment-defending ministers.

We all have our little prejudices, our little oversimplifications. And if the task of the Church is to "go into all the world and preach the gospel and heal the sick," then maybe we should at least be grateful that Campus Crusade and Inter-Varsity, and Young Life, and the Healing Order of St. Luke are doing it. At least they have a plan. At least they have a vision and are trying to fulfill it.

Are you "traditionalists" trying? Are you faith-buriers in the game, on the field, fighting the good fight? If you've got a better way to tell about Jesus, I'm sure Billy Graham would like to know it!

The trouble with the traditionalists is that they are like salesmen who never ask the customer to sign on the line! Your mainline church men are salesmen who are forever cultivating the prospect, but always afraid to "put the question." Maybe by putting the question you do offend a few. Maybe it will get too close for some people's comfort. Many a time the Master did exactly that! But somehow, somewhere, you've got to try. Even if you get yourself crucified.

Of course, you may win the crown of life. You may find a life, with Jesus, like nothing you've ever known before. You may just change the whole world.

Have your denominations, your traditions, if you want them. But have Christ first. Keep him at the heart: of your church, of your tradition, but most of all — of your own life.

That's when your investment will pay off. That's when your gamble will win. That's when the Kingdom will come. The decision is yours to make — tonight.

The Parable Of The Sower (Soil)

"Listen! A sower went out to sow. And as he sowed, some seed fell along the path ... other seed fell on rocky ground ... other seed fell among thorns ... and other seeds fell into good soil and brought forth grain."
— Mark 4:3, 5, 7, 8

I

The Devil's Advocate:

Mr. Sower — the soil is now ready.
In the Church there are more than a few
All eager — all anxious — all expectant.
Your good listeners are waiting for you!

You bet they are, Mr. Sower. They're waiting, all right. Look at them. Asleep, grumpy, anxious to be sure, worn-out, bored, saturated with good things, hardened, toughened, preoccupied with other things.

But to tell you the truth, I'm on their side. And I am sure that most of you out there are secretly on my side. I know you are a little reluctant to admit it in front of the preacher. I know he holds a certain sway over your conscience. He is sort of a father-image for you, and you don't want to disappoint him, at least to his face. But you know, and I know, that deep down, you really see things as I see them. And that's all I care about. So long as down deep you hang on to the same things I do.

Now in a few minutes he'll have to have his say. And in piously warm, personalistic tones, he'll try to persuade you to be good soil, soft and pliable, open and receptive to his message. And he'll use every method imaginable. He'll wink at the impressionable young women. He'll call up the memories of your faithful mother and father. He'll try to con you into thinking tenderly of the hard realities of life. So right now, you can prepare yourself for the emotional onslaught.

Preachers are emotional because of their naïveté. You can expect him to tell us we ought not to be hardened like the *path* in the parable. He'll want us to be soft and pliable and open. But you and I know that to be a lot of nonsense. Listen, this world is not a place for softies! This is a time for hardened people, tough people, people who know what they want and who do not open themselves up for all the religious twaddle that issues out of pulpits.

Listen, 10,000 voices are clamoring to be heard today. Everybody is screaming at you, telling you your car is out of date, your furniture out of style, that you have bad breath, or that you need to use a stronger deodorant. Pictures, billboards, articles, ads, commercials shout at you.

Yippy, yappy hippies yelled through their beards and long hair that you were a bigoted, hypocritical, middle-class warmongering s.o.b. Arrogant, indulged, spoiled affluent brats drive away to college in BMWs and miniskirts that their parents bought for them and then write in the campus newspaper that their parents are a bunch of phony, double-standard materialists.

Then the executives of major communications networks decide they're going to puff up questionable celebrities and political activists. So every other night we hear these blowhard nonleaders tell us where we're wrong; that we're not only responsible for our own sins, but *theirs* too. With all that screaming and shouting, who wouldn't be hardened?

So, I'm with you. You have to harden yourself to the many voices and philosophies of today. Otherwise, you'll just disintegrate. Keep hard and resolute.

In this case, I think Sigmund Freud was right. Here, in the words of Gerald Sykes, is what he might say to us today:

> *Get clear about your relations to your mother and father, your brothers and sisters, and all the rest of your family ...*

Understand the power of the death instinct.

See the sexual truth about yourself, and don't be stupidly ashamed of it. Face up to the ghastly sordidness, the disgusting vulgarity of being a human being — and your reward will be that you will have the answers *while your softheaded contemporaries are merely fooling around with words.*

Traps are being laid for you every day. A great swindle called either by the name of a church or of a political system or some other institution is seeking every second to take you in with its calming mythology. You can beat the game — and enjoy the infinite satisfaction of watching the great majority crawl on its belly toward you. All you need is to be clear and strong.[1]

The Lord's Advocate:

Ah! The sirens of Scylla and Charybdis: how they woo us to the shoals of self-interest and success. Cry on, Devil man: you talk to us all, and you're right, we give you a hearing, every one of us in our secret hearts.

We'd love to think the world would crawl to us: that by some secret Nietzchean knowledge we could exploit the sin of our souls and society's soul and turn it into profit for ourselves. We might even con our consciences for a while. But not for long, I think. Somewhere, out there, there is a longing for life — real life, a hunger for the highest, a tension until the truth be found.

Let me concede your point about preachers. We do delude ourselves. We are vain, pompous, and proud little people. Because we are human — and it is our shame. Only by God's mercy will most of us find our way into the Kingdom.

But you cannot curse the message by the man. For we proclaim not ourselves but Christ Jesus. And in this marvelous parable of the Master's you're dealing not with the likes of me, but with the Lord himself. Remember he is the Sower, and it is his Word that is the seed being scattered.

Say what you will about the fraudulent faces of us who proclaim the faith. Mouth all the old excuses church members themselves have used for why their lives are too hard for the hope of heaven to find root within their souls! But when you're face to face with the Sower who is the Savior, you'll not fault him! Look to yourself, Devil man! And you people look to yourselves, and who you're letting in your heart — the Divine Lord, or this Devil-friend.

He wants you to think "hardness of heart" is a virtue, very modern, "cool," cosmopolitan, the thing. Be tough in a tough world.

If you're hard men, it's because you've let everything walk up and down your life — every "passing wind of doctrine," every new bit of gossip, every lewd picture, every cruel thought, every cheap, unworthy idea that came traveling down the pike.

One of the beautiful prayers of the faith says, "Let not our hearts be busy inns."

Maybe you've been busy, busy, busy with a thousand things each day. Maybe you're so important you really haven't time to take a look at Christ's way. I know the newspaper seems much more important at seven o'clock in the morning than a chapter out of John or Mark. But will it be with you to help some day when you face the dark?

It will not. Neither will the fare you found on television late into the night — nor the conversation of your friends — all of which you put before the cry to cultivate the cutting edge and growing life of prayer, and the discipline of devoted reading of the Bible. They are seed for the soil that the heart and mind full of the garbage of the day is too sated to satisfy.

Is your heart really that hard? I think it's not!

II

The Devil's Advocate:

No matter how you say it, I think most of us come off rather badly in this parable. It is unfair to us. Now, you take that bit about the rocky soil. You know what kind of soil that is? It's soil that's about an inch thick with a solid layer of rock underneath. Like the parable says, it's hard to put deep roots down in that kind of soil.

But that's not so bad — at least not from our point of view. We've already agreed that you've got to be hard in this life. That's what's important. Now, of course, some people think you should add a little surface softness, an appearance of kindness and receptivity, a diplomatic disposition to make human relationships more palatable. I see nothing wrong in that.

And I notice most of you feel the same way. You are basically hard as rock underneath. You can resist a whole mountain of verbiage, ward off the onslaught of 1,000 salesmen and preachers. But you are very clever and cunning. You come to church because it's easier that way. It's an accepted thing to do. Life is calmer when you do. The folks back home think it looks good. And the genteel, moral influence of church can certainly do no harm. It makes the wife happier. Besides that, it ceases the twinge of conscience we might have if we didn't attend.

So in the nice, pleasant, amiable surroundings of the church we all develop a nice, pleasant, amiable personality. And I'm for it. Things go better that way. But I must say that some of you get carried away with the whole thing and pretend you are enthusiastic about religion. Of course, you and I know you don't mean it and that it's only the fun thing to do at the time. However, there is this matter of excess, you know. Some of you are even claiming new birth and conversion.

Don't you think that's being just a bit too amiable? You could get on quite well in the church and society without getting all lathered up about your love for Jesus. You know that can't last. Not in our kind of world. So my advice is to keep up the surface niceness, the affability and amiability. But never let down your rock-like defenses. You know that all those nice religious sentiments will never make it in our kind of world.

Just take a look around at all these Jesus fulminators. They give you all that sweet-syrup stuff about giving the heart to Jesus. Well, don't believe it. I'm convinced they are basically just like you and me — rock-hardened underneath. I've heard them backbite, gossip, expound their ignorance ad nauseam, consign everyone else to hell, and judge everyone else's beliefs and doctrines by their own simplistic formulas. They are full of pride. They have Messianic complexes. They are determined to make everyone go through their kind of religious experience just so they can have psychological power over other people.

Now I ask you, isn't that like the rest of us? They claim to be soft and pliable and receptive to the Word of God. But look at them closely and you'll find a super-huge, extra-hard ego covered over with the "Four Spiritual Laws" of Campus Crusade and Billy Graham clichés.

So don't waste your energy. Don't have religious flare-ups. Be cool. Be hard. That's the only way to survive all the windy nonsense.

The Lord's Advocate:

You have a thin blade, Lucifer ... and you know just how to slit it in between the ribs and twist it.

Better to be false, eh? Better to be soft and pliable on the surface but like a rock within? I do believe you are the father of fraud! You and your subtle insinuations are the hometown of hypocrisy!

Because it's a mellow voice with which you croon. Not a few of our forces would love to think that just what you propose is okay! Particularly if they could have all the words that sound just right: all the talk about the gospel, and about Jesus, and about conversion, and walking with the Lord, but still have the aura of affluence that a place in Prestigeville offers! What could be better, after all, than to have your Jesus Christ on Sunday — full-fledged, and foursquare gospel — and your cocktails at the club, and cigars after dinner, and that sense of worldly involvement all through the week?

It could make Docetists of us: people who take our pleasures where we find them, and say no bodily excesses interfere with the purity of the Spirit. Live a little! That's all right! The Lord doesn't mind! Have a hard heart underneath! Make sanctity a thing of the surface for the sake of society.

Sure, there are some who consciously live like that. There are hypocrites in the world and in the church — we all have trouble with the beam in our own eye when we're worrying about the speck in our brother's.

But I do not know many who want to live that way. Most of those I know are in the church out of deep hunger and longing need. They have no desire to be false.

But they are tempted, and sometimes trapped: we all are tempted to come to Christ for all the wrong reasons: because he, in his singing, swinging, free-moving life is the most glamorous personality they've come across in these times full of tired and tedious types.

Some move in with the Christian crowd just to make friends, or because joining a church is good company policy: image, you know. Some think, especially in the suburbs, that they'll be safe away from the sordid sorrows and stubborn sicknesses of the city. They never think the Lord Jesus would be so impertinent as to protrude himself into their consciences out there. And, of course, when the kitchen gets hot, and they see the Lord means business with their lives, and that it's not a talking game, anymore, but a *living* game, then they take their marbles and play elsewhere.

But I believe the ones who care come back. Christ's own are not lost. And they're not the shallow soil with the rock beneath, and they want no part of it.

So go away, you apostle of insinuation, and take your gravel with you.

III

The Devil's Advocate:

Now this next part of the parable is where a lot of people get bamboozled. You know, the part where the thorns choke out the good grain. And of course, Mark tells us the thorns represent the cares of the world, the delight of riches, and the desire for other things.

I have noticed that once in a while some of our hardest, sturdiest, most stable types begin to fall for this one. It often happens, as Vance Packard points out in his book, *The Pyramid Climbers*, to men in their forties and fifties. He says that life, in the thirty-year-olds in our businesses and corporations, seems amazingly simple. They see the world as demanding intelligent achievement, and they intend to achieve no matter what. They are grey flannel suit types. They are out there to succeed, to make the buck as quickly as possible.

But men in their *forties* begin to wonder if the objectives of their organizations are correct. Packard says that they begin "to re-examine their own inner lives and personal desires." Sometimes they wonder if they "should not have chosen some other occupation, one they propose as more attuned to human values, to the rewards of interpersonal relations."[2]

The fifty-year-olds become philosophic, and usually try to rationalize their lifelong devotion to the goddess of success. And even though they tend to prattle on in nostalgic reconstructions of their successes and even though they sound like repetitious windbags to the juniors who work under them, we must affirm them to be right. Their position is ultimately the correct one.

It is correct because it is the only realistic one. There *is* delight in riches! And the cares of business which bring a handsome profit are happily endured for the reward. The parable has it wrong. *Riches* are not thorns, they are flowers — flowers yielding sweet-scented fragrances and delights and pleasures.

Now look at the poor. Do you think they enjoy their diets of malnutrition? Do you think they are happy with only one car and a house furnished from garage sales and Goodwill instead of prestigious furniture stores? Not on your life! Do you think they enjoy sitting home sipping beer and watching videos? Not a bit. They would all unquestionably enjoy cocktails and beef at the best restaurants, theater in New York, and blintzes at the Carnegie Deli. Listen, they want to be right where you are. So don't give anyone a chance to delude you with nice religious folderol.

Most religious guys are phonies anyway. They talk against riches and success, but, brother, they'll take it any day. They'll tsk, tsk us with a holier-than-thou attitude because we're out there fighting for financial success. Yet, have you noticed? They'll take every penny we give them.

So if the "thorns" of riches and desires and worldly cares choke out the so-called Word of God, it's only because riches and desires are *real* and the Word of God is not.

The Lord's Advocate:

Are they ever real! To all of us they're real. We do like our cars and ski-doos, our gracious homes and wide lawns. We like our clothes and clubs.

But Christ's concern was *how much* we like them, whether we give our loyalty and love to them. Whether they dominate and control us. Whether they, in fact, are god to us. That's what he saw in the Rich Young Man — that he couldn't give it up. And that was the Savior's sorrow; for he wanted that young man. He loved him. And knew that he could have come, if his heart had been willing to let his wealth go.

Men can be wealthy without being worldly. Men can have riches and still stand for the right. It's a question of who and what is God to you.

You just check out your giving to Christ's cause, to see just how chained you may be to the riches you have. You know, even a tip isn't ten percent anymore! You might see whether you're trying just to tip your Lord instead of really rising up to follow him, using your riches for the redeeming of the world. With a few magnificent exceptions it is rather revealing that the ratio of people's giving to the church goes down as they get richer.

Maybe it is harder for those who trust in riches to get into the Kingdom of Heaven, than for a camel to go through the eye of a needle! Maybe the thorns of wealth, and ambition, and prestige, and success, and suburban isolation from the sufferings of society — and all the other trappings of *white power*, really do choke out the growing flowers of God's love from our hearts and his care from our consciences — unless we're in there every day with the plow of prayer, and the hoe of the regular hearing of God's Word on Sunday, and the hoeing of the scriptures.

Sure, the weeds are there — but it's flowers, for those of faith.

IV

The Devil's Advocate:

Now this last part of the parable is just too much. Have you ever heard such nonsense? Do you see what the climax to this story is? It suggests that the soft, open, pliable types are the real producers. They are the ones who reap the rewards.

I'm sure you agree with me that only the gullible could believe that bundle of twaddle. Look around you. Who is it that really makes it in this world? Who is it that really has success? It's the hardheaded hustlers who know the realities of economic life. Oh, sure, they may look soft but they play hard. They'll tell you that themselves. It's a hard game out there. It's a rat race, they say. And they are right.

Most all of us believe that, don't we? Sure we do! However, once in a while some of us wonder about it all; we wonder if the struggle is worth it all, and if we shouldn't turn our attention to other things like, say, religion. But you know what that is, don't you? That's the rationalization of a man who's not making it in the economic world. He's just nursing his wounds and bruises with religious consolation. He needs encouragement and he would take it from anybody — even God.

Oh, well, that's okay. We all know that once he's on his feet again, he'll be his old hard self and resist the religious sentimentalisms. Unless, of course, he continues to fall. Then he'll either be religious or alcoholic or both. And the only thing he'll produce thirty-, sixty-, or a hundredfold, is trouble. But you and I, we'll continue in our push for the fruits of success in this world. It's the only thing that counts.

The Lord's Advocate:

Not the only thing that counts, my friend: not when your back's to the wall, and you're in a corner, and the clouds are rolling in, and death walks your way, and tragedy snaps at your heels. Not then, it isn't all that counts!

About all it does is pay the funeral costs, or the medical bills, or the psychiatrist's fees: it doesn't heal anything. It doesn't help anything. It doesn't even buy a friend.

What shines a light when all is dark; what brings up the sun when the night's been long; what heals the heart that's been horribly hurt; what provides an answer when the spirit is numb; what provides a highway of hope when there is no escape — is something in the heart. In your heart. In Everyman's heart, who hungers for the highest.

And that is faith. And faith means Christ the Lord — Christ of the Cross, Christ of the crown. His victory is hard. It is through the rain to the sun beyond. It is through the tears to the day of Triumph. And it's the way he offers us.

It's the way open to those whose heart is a field prayerful enough for plowing, hopeful enough for the harvest.

It's the way of the Lord for those who hear and believe that God loved the world so much, that he gave his only begotten Son, that they might not perish but have life and have it more abundantly.

The soft winds of the world have winsome voices — but you listen for the winds of God that come whistling down the highways of the heart for those who hear the Word of their Lord Jesus, and know that they are called to be good soil — deep, rich, ready!

---

1. Gerald Sykes, *The Hidden Remnant* (New York: Harper), p. 50.

2. Vance Packard, *The Pyramid Climbers*, Crest Book reprint (Greenwich, Connecticut: Faucett Publications, 1964), pp. 198-199.

The Wicked Husbandmen

He had still one other, a beloved son, finally he sent him to them, saying, "They will respect my son." But those tenants said to one another, "This is the heir, let us kill him" ... What will the owner of the vineyard do? He will destroy the tenants and give the vineyard to others. — Mark 12:6-7, 9

I

The Devil's Advocate:

Well, Mr. Lord's Advocate and fellow hypocrites, this is my last time to be with you discussing the parables. I must say that these discussions have been a delight for me. I always welcome the chance for further elucidation of my views. And it has been most rewarding to find such a sympathetic reception among your people. In fact, I often feel that I can call them my people.

This parable is most interesting. As I see it, the parable has to do with stewardship and ownership. But more than that, it has to do with absentee ownership — something which my opponent must certainly not advocate, for he frequently rails against the absentee landlords of the slum properties. So tonight's story is about an absentee landlord and his claims on his property and how his property should be treated.

The parable is so explicit that it could be called an allegory. It is obvious that the vineyard represents the people of Israel, for as the prophet Isaiah said long before, "The vineyard of the Lord is the house of Israel." The owner of the vineyard is God, and the cultivators are the religious leaders of Israel who had charge of the religious welfare of their people. The messengers represent the prophets who were sent by God. And, of course, the only son who was killed by the cultivators or tenants was Jesus Christ.

As usual, my opponent will try to twist this parable, or allegory, for his own purposes. He will support the idea of absentee landlordship and even go so far as to claim that there is such a thing as a heavenly landlord.

But I want you to know that if there is such a thing as a heavenly landlord, he is certainly an absentee one. He claims ownership of everything, but have you ever seen him? The tenants had the right idea. Even if there is such a thing as an absentee landlord, there shouldn't be. So they acted to take over what was properly theirs.

The Lord's Advocate:

Mr. Devil's Advocate, you overpower me with your arguments. You are all over the board, checkmating all efforts to make sense for the Savior. Maybe, for self-sufficient modern man, the Jesus way just doesn't make sense! In fact, last night, as I sat nodding in my chair, trying to think of something to say to you, I concluded that you are unbeatable. After all, we should give the Devil his due, as the fellow says. In short, it seemed, I must concede!

You win, Mr. Devil's Advocate. You are well known around here. You do have many a secret admirer — if not any open converts! We like your flair — the way you dare to go just anywhere to sow your insinuations, to spread your sin, to make men think that they can win anything and everything.

It certainly swells their egos and inflates their pride: "I am the captain of my ship — I am the master of my fate."

Take the landlord thing. Absentee landlordism is evil. If, in being absent, the landlord does nothing for his renters: lets the toilets clog and the lights go out.

But do you think the Lord was such a one? Jesus does not say the landlord cheated his tenants, that he let the place go to rack and ruin. That he overcharged and underserved.

He just said the tenants were using his farm, and didn't pay up. It was his farm, his world, his kingdom. After all, you're the great free enterpriser, the maker of self-made men! Why should not men on the make pay their rent?

Turn simple injustice and premeditated murder into rightful possession by those who have the power to extort at will, and you've succeeded in making evil good, and black white, and I congratulate you — and I concede!

II

The Devil's Advocate:

Well! Thank you very much! Now if the servant or messengers in this parable represent the prophets that have been sent to Israel, Jesus may have had in mind someone like Amos. And Amos is a perfect example of the point I wish to make.

Amos lived and preached and wrote around 750 B.C.E. He directed his message against the Northern Kingdom, Israel. Now, you think he would leave them alone. Israel had prospered wonderfully. Their capital city, Samaria, was a beautiful place set on a hill. Many people had both winter and summer houses, built substantially of cut stone. They enjoyed such luxuries as carved ivories and delicate foods. Business was booming and the city was strongly fortified. Who could ask for more? The Great Society had arrived.

But now listen to old Amos, the religious spoilsport, as he comes and attempts to ruin it all. He says:

Woe to those who are at ease in Zion,
and to those who feel secure on the
mountains of Samaria.
Woe to those who lie upon beds of ivory,
and stretch themselves upon their couches ...
Who sing idle songs to the sound of the harp,
and like David invent for themselves
instruments of music,
Who drink wine in bowls,
and anoint themselves with the finest oils,
but are not grieved over the ruin of Joseph!

Do you see my point? He was unable to enjoy life. He felt guilty over the good life when it came, just as many of you feel guilty — with your wealth. But that is nonsense.

Let me tell you something else. Amos was a southerner and he was preaching in a northern city. In the first place, he was an outsider. And in the second place, he had a southern accent. Besides all that, he was not even a professional speaker or writer. He was an unsophisticated farmer trying to speak to the sophisticated people of Samaria.

He just wasn't with it. He didn't understand the new ways. He had never experienced the delights of wealth and sophisticated living. Amos was unacquainted with real life. He was jealous.

Is it any wonder they asked him to go back to the farm and preach there? He tried to claim that everything they had belonged to God. But the people knew that it was their own political and economic skill that had gotten them where they were. And they weren't going to give it up to the claims of some so-called absentee landlord. It was theirs. So go back home, Amos, and take care of your cheap sheep and sycamore trees.

The Lord's Advocate:

Cheap sheep and sycamore trees maybe: but at least it was close to the land. At least he knew "summer and winter, springtime and harvest." At least he knew the rising of the sun and the going down of the same!

Country-man, yes; and with an eye that could scan the horizon of the hills for a lost sheep, but could also scan the horizons of the heart and find lost men. Uncanny crofter from the country!

Maybe he was embarrassed and offended by wealth, especially when he saw rich men doing others in by stealth, and saw them rolling in riches while the poor perished.

How can we sleep when others have no beds? How can we eat when others have no food? How can we live in luxury when others lie in lonely slums waiting for death's deliverance?

Oh, sure, I understand their rejecting a prophet like Amos. They could not live with their consciences as long as he was there. Only when you dare to give it up can you look life in the eye and say, "I, too, once wanted pie in the sky by and by," but "I live for Jesus now, and have new life. For my life is God's: and all my goods are God's. And I am glad to share and help people be aware that they are my brothers and sisters."

We're not so different, are we? Who is more "at ease in Zion" than we, in our idyllic suburbs? Who wants to think about starvation in Africa when we had meatloaf or roast beef or chicken today — and vegetables, bread, butter, tea, and cookies?

Oh, no, it takes a man to come and tell us we cannot rest until we have built Jerusalem in this, our green and pleasant land.

And if he troubles our consciences, and makes us join the army of the Lord and enter into the battle of life and fight for the right — so much the better!

Any takers?

III

The Devil's Advocate:

Not many, I'll bet! According to Jesus' parable, one or two other messengers were sent to the people of Israel. They too were supposed to represent some prophets. Let us imagine that one of them might have been Jeremiah. He came on the scene about 626 B.C.E. He was from the south, but at least he did his preaching and teaching in the south. So at least he had that in his favor. He didn't go meddling in other people's business. But he certainly meddled in the business of his own people.

Let me tell you a little more about this man, Jeremiah. He was from a family of priests. He came from a small village outside Jerusalem, but it wasn't long until Jeremiah knew his way around Jerusalem. In fact, quite soon he became an insider, a man well acquainted with the Jerusalem Establishment.

Jeremiah was not a rustic rube like Amos. He was a cultured, sophisticated man of the city. Familiar with the political and economic realities of Jerusalem and the whole Southern Kingdom, Jeremiah could not be accused, like Amos, of not knowing the score. Just the contrary, Jeremiah was "in the know."

That's why his activity is so hard to understand. He was one of the "in-crowd"; he had it made in the power structure and its society. Yet, he began to speak out against that very power structure. He began to criticize his own establishment. He accused the priests and prophets of phoniness and fakery. He began knocking the alleged hypocrisy of some of his cronies in the Downtown Club of Jerusalem.

Listen to a few of Jeremiah's more juicy pronouncements:

An appalling and horrible thing
has happened in the land:
The prophets prophesy falsely,
and the priests rule at their direction;
My people love to have it so,
but what will you do when the end comes?

And in another place:

For from the least to the greatest of them,
everyone is greedy for unjust gain;
And from prophet to priest,
everyone deals falsely.
They have healed the wound of my people lightly,
saying, "Peace, peace
when there is no peace."

And yet again, Jeremiah says:

Cursed is the man who trusts in man
and makes flesh his arm,
whose heart turns away from the Lord.

But who else can you trust in than man? Your Lord is not around. He is an absentee, remember! So Jeremiah begins to repudiate his buddies. The very people he had come to love and trust, he now excoriates. And why? Just because they practiced a little favoritism among each other at the expense of the poor?

Then Jeremiah went way too far. He even hoped for the destruction of his country so that some of his religious notions of judgment and repentance might be met. Is it any wonder that they locked him up? He was a dangerously religious fanatic and traitor.

Yet, Jesus condones that sort of person in his parable. I think the tenants, the husbandmen, had a right to stone the messengers. They were nuts, mad, possessed. There was no absentee landlord up in the sky. Such a concept was only perverted, inflamed imagination of the religious fanatics. And yet again, Jeremiah says:

Cursed is the man who trusts in man
and makes flesh his arm,
whose heart turns away from the Lord.

But who else can you trust in than man? Your Lord is not around. He is an absentee, remember!

The Lord's Advocate:

Well, the religious men of zeal have never had much appeal, have they? We don't like to be exposed. We don't like to be caught with our emotions down, and our heart showing, do we?

I'm interested that the prophets puzzle even you, Mr. Devil's Advocate. You really don't like religious enthusiasm, do you? I suppose when people begin to feel really wholehearted about their faith, and begin to talk about the Lord, and to sing and shout their enthusiasm, and to be earnest in their faith, you become really quite nervous. That's when you begin to lose your grip on my people, isn't it?

It's funny how much we all are like those tenant farmers. We forget the world we live in has been given to us, that we are trespassers in God's domain. We forget we're borrowers of everything we have. And what God asks back is very little. But how we do begrudge God's claim on us! We do not want to owe him anything, and it is a shock to think, in fact, we owe him everything.

And we do not like to be told. We particularly do not like our own kind telling us — people as educated as we are, people as cultured as we are, people as widely traveled as we are, people as acquainted with the good things of life as we are: people who have every reason to be self-centered and self-serving as we are! When they, the sophisticates, the cosmopolitans, begin to needle the establishment, and speak up against its sins and blindness, it's one of our own doing us in and that hatred is so close to love, that revenge lies so close to the surface — and retaliation becomes a terrible temptation!

So Jeremiah was even less forgivable than Amos. An ignorant shepherd you can excuse. But what can you do with a Harvard man, or a Union Seminary man — but trap him if you can. Charge him with turning against his own — even against his fellow-clergy — when he accuses them with:

> *They have healed the wounds of my people*
> *lightly saying, "Peace, peace,*
> *when there is no peace."*

Jesus was so right: God's children, who owed him everything, killed the prophets when they were sent to them, because they did not want to hear the truth. How many here tonight have hearts humble enough to hear the truth, and believe, and accept the Lord, and accept his messengers, and give back to God what is his due?

That is the test — and you'll know who's yours among these people, Mr. Devil-Man, by how each one's colors fly on this question.

IV

The Devil's Advocate:

Now the last guy in this parable, the beloved son, undoubtedly represents Jesus, who was purported to be the Son of God. According to the story, the absentee landlord decides to send the son, thinking the tenants will listen to him.

But the tenants are too smart for that. They could see a troublemaker a mile away. After all, hadn't they heard those prophetic types before? They knew all about Amos and Jeremiah and the others. Jesus sounded just like them. He claimed that the earth and its people belonged to God, and that they ought to give him his due in worship and obedience.

However, it's all rather funny, because Jesus alienated the very people who could have helped him most. First of all, he alienated the Pharisees by breaking some of their most important religious rules, such as not working on the Sabbath. He further displeased them by associating with poor people, with half-breed Samaritans, and with prostitutes and tax collectors. In their eyes, therefore, Jesus was not religious enough to be God's Son and special messenger.

Secondly, Jesus alienated the Sadducees, who were mainly the priests, by criticizing their Temple. The Temple was, of course, the very center of their religion and nation and culture. Yet Jesus claimed that the place of worship was relatively unimportant, because God was a Spirit, and should therefore be worshiped in spirit and truth. Furthermore, Jesus predicted that the Temple would be destroyed, and he acted almost as if he didn't care if it was. Imagine the fury that caused with the Sadducees and the whole Jewish nation.

So it was that Jesus had the religious leaders against him — the very people whom you would think would have been his strongest allies. But he just continued to alienate them by claiming they themselves had been lousy stewards of religion. Is it any wonder they killed him?

Well, in conclusion, I must say that I am delighted that most of you feel that way about Jesus too. This is not God's world. It is our world. God has no right to collect anything from us even if he does exist. We have to make it on our own. If God is, he isn't here. He's an absentee landlord. Anybody acquainted with the slums knows the absentee landlord cares nothing about the tenants. The only interest he has in them is the money they pay him for rent.

So Jesus had no right to make such radical, fanatical claims. He got what was coming to him. He was trying to upset everything — our whole political, economical, and yes, even our religious system. Things were going well until the likes of him and Amos and Jeremiah came along. They disturbed everything so there's no peace anymore. But you and I know it is our world, our life, our future, and no absentee God has any business making claim on us.

The Lord's Advocate:

If it is our world, and God has no part in it, why can we not run it by ourselves? Why do our human plans go wrong? Why is there trial and error? Why are "the best-laid plans of mice and men" so often foiled?

No, it's not our world. Even at our most powerful, we do not control it. We are human — merely human. And we die. Even the great and good among us die.

No — it is only when we in our deepest hearts are in tune with God that we come even close to controlling our world, having power in our world, and taming and using and triumphing through and over our world. And anyone who's ever really been up against it, or who, on the other hand, has ever sat dwarfed and spellbound in a lone canoe on a northern lake, beneath the great arch of the heavens and looked up at the silent stars, knows that it's Someone Else's world, someone who has a secret, whose power he can share only when we learn that secret.

And I say, Mr. Devil's Advocate, in spite of your cackling, offstage laughter, that learning that secret is the one ultimate thing humanity is about. Trying to find out what's with this God of the universe, and how, in heaven's name, we can ever screw up the courage to trust that God! That's what living is! That's what growing up is. That's what maturing and becoming wise really is! Learning the humility to "become as a little child" and trust God.

And the tragedy of those tenant farmers is that, like so many people today, they thought they were going to get away with something by shortcutting and short circuiting the law, and human responsibility and certainly love, by doing in those whom they thought stood between them and easy street!

And a tragedy doubly-compounded when the last messenger they did in — the heir himself — was the one man of all the messengers who came with forgiveness and "healing in his wings," who was "the man for others," the man for them, the man who ultimately, through their deed of treachery, actually laid down his life for them. By Jesus' own words, there is no greater love than that!

He pointed the finger, and prodded the conscience, and grieved over them because they needed to face the accusing finger: they needed to repent in order to be healed and forgiven! It was their chance of a lifetime. And they botched it. And only in hell would they ever know how badly they had botched it!

You can say Jesus got what was coming to him. And the wicked husbandmen got what was coming to them! Indeed, they determined what was coming to them. They asked for it — destruction and rejection.

But that isn't what the Landlord wanted for them. That isn't what God wanted for them. He sent his Son, with life and with love.

My friends, our Antagonist here would make you wicked husbandmen, too! Narrow, self-centered, self-serving, self-gratifying sinners, too! He'd suck you down to death with all the others in all the ages who have wanted only to serve and to save themselves.

Let me tell you. They all lost. And he lost them. And he wants to send you there too — if you'll let him "sell" you.

It's no deal! No deal for people who are God's sons and daughters, and who have a rightful heritage as God's children to claim. And the way you claim it is by identifying, accepting, signing up with Jesus. He is the last messenger, who comes to us, the tenant-farmers, to collect the rent.

Do you know what it is? Just your life, that's all. Just your heart, for Jesus. Give him that, and the whole blooming vineyard is yours — life is yours, love is yours, hope is yours, daily help is yours.

I dare you to pay the rent, tonight!

www.ingramcontent.com/pod-product-compliance
Lightning Source LLC
LaVergne TN
LVHW020658100826
845148LV00012B/2550

9780788019395